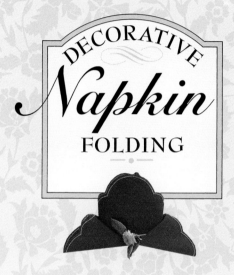

DECORATIVE

Napkin

FOLDING

Managing Editor: Jo Finnis
Design and typesetting: Stonecastle Graphics Ltd
Photography: Nelson Hargreaves
Production: Ruth Arthur, Sally Connolly, Neil Randles,
Karen Staff and Jonathan Tickner
Director of Production: Gerald Hughes

CHARTWELL BOOKS
A division of Book Sales, Inc.
POST OFFICE BOX 7100
114 Northfield Avenue
Edison, NJ 08837

CLB 4302
© 1994 CLB Publishing,
Godalming, Surrey, U.K.
Printed and bound in Singapore
ISBN 0-7858-0374-2

DECORATIVE
Napkin
FOLDING

PAMELA
WESTLAND

CHARTWELL
BOOKS, INC

A crisply-starched cotton napkin folded to represent a dainty slipper for a wedding-day table; a bright jade cotton square ringed around with sunshine yellow, springtime blossoms; a red and white gingham napkin folded envelope-style to contain a place setting of cutlery, or elegant peach-coloured damask napkin rolled, pleated and tied with a contrasting moiré ribbon band - whatever your style and whatever the occasion, the way you present your table napkins plays a significant part in setting the scene.

A glance at the step-by-step photographs throughout the book will show you how easy it is to present table napkins simply, yet with flair and style; how to fold napkins into symbolic or representational shapes such as the rising sun or a butterfly; how to create other designs to enclose a flower, a posy, a tiny gift or a secondary napkin. Yet more styles are designed to be purely inspirational - to illustrate that a hoop of fresh flowers or herbs, a bangle of beads or even candies can be just as effective and sometimes more fun than any conventional napkin ring.

Take care that your table napkins match the mood of the occasion. Brightly-coloured cotton ones set the scene for a bistro- or trattoria-style meal; lace-trimmed table napkins add a touch of glamour and nostalgia, and crisp damask or linen ones in the 'dinner' size (65 cm/25 in square) signify that you are putting on the style. But then paper napkins can do that too. If you want your table layout to be a sensation and linen stocks are low, see how, in two of our photographs, paper tableware can rise to the dressiest of occasions.

Practise any one of several folds on table napkins of all kinds and you will find that the designs are just as effective whether they are created with the finest lace or the brightest cotton. One factor they do all have in common: plain or fancy, the napkins must be freshly laundered, carefully ironed (neat corners are particulary important) and lightly spray-starched.

Above: You can trim simple folds and further enhance fancy ones with a variety of natural and decorative materials, from herbs and spices, flowers and leaves to tassels and braid, ribbons and beads.

Right: Printed cottons and fine linens, appliqué and lace, paper napkins and transparent ones, these are the stuff that decorative napkin foldings are made of.

The double envelope folding of a white damask napkin is parted at the centre to take a small gift of wrapped chocolates, exquisitely presented in circles of net tied dolly-bag style.

1 Fold the napkin into three, then make a small pleat down the centre of the top layer.

2 Turn the napkin over and fold it under twice from each end, so that the edges meet in the centre.

3 Pull up the top layer of one of the side panels and pinch the two edges together to make a diamond shape.

4 Tuck the centre point of the diamond under the pleat. Fold and tuck in the other three panels in a similar way.

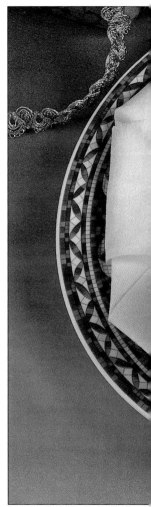

Above: Two opposite corners of the napkin are turned in, then it is rolled, starting from one of the exposed points. Wire-edged ribbon is folded into pleats to decorate one edge, and tied into a bow to trim the small gift parcel.

The delicate lace corner panel on a cream linen napkin is shown at its prettiest in this cascade design, which may be displayed vertically with the pleats held in a wine glass or napkin ring.

1 Fold the napkin in half diagonally to make a triangle, then fold over the two right-angled points to make a boat shape.

2 Starting at one end, make even accordion pleats about 4 cm/1^1/$_2$ in wide all along the length of the napkin.

3 Holding the napkin by the bottom edge, open out the pleats so that they cascade at the sides.

Left: A less formal presentation of the waterfall fold is achieved with a cotton napkin in deep, rich purple. With the pleats held in a bone napkin ring, there is scope for the addition of a small posy or a single flower.

There is a hint of the dervishes in this exuberant design, created by first pleating then tightly rolling the napkin. The skill, and the style, are in the final arrangement, when the pleats are fanned out into a swirl.

1 Fold the napkin into three, then fold it in half diagonally.

2 Tightly roll up the long strip, starting from one short end. Tuck in the end underneath the roll.

3 Ease up the centre to form a mound, then fan out the pleats.

Above: The printed napkin is folded, then tightly rolled around the chopsticks, while the rust-coloured napkin is folded diagonally and then knotted around the breadsticks.

In Victorian times this dainty fold, known as the lady's slipper, was popular to decorate the tables at wedding and christening feasts.

1 Fold the napkin into four to form a small square, then fold it over to make a triangle with the decorative edges on top.

2 Fold the two sides inwards so that the edges meet vertically at the centre. Fold under the two flaps at the base to make a triangle.

3 Fold the triangle in half with the flaps tucked inwards. Hold it at the base and pull up each of the four points in turn.

Below: A dainty green napkin with a lily-of-the-valley design is simply held in a band of pearl beads and scattered with romantic rose petals.

A napkin with a scalloped edge furthers the illusion
in this butterfly design, which is enhanced by
the addition of pink and
purple primroses.

1 Fold over the two side edges of the napkin to meet along the centre. Fold it in half horizontally to make a long, narrow strip.

2 Make a pleat in the left-hand end of the rectangle, so that the fold reaches the centre. Repeat on the other side.

3 Beginning at the left-hand side, crease the top two layers of the fold to form a triangle and fold them flat. Open out and fold the next two layers to make another triangle, then fold these layers flat.

4 Repeat on the other side. Open out the wings to form a butterfly shape.

Left: A silk butterfly decoration and a toning ribbon complement a plain peach napkin presented in a simple triangular fold.

Two napkins in peach and apricot colours become horns of plenty, spilling over with fruits, flowers and ears of wheat for a seasonal table centrepiece.

1 Fold the napkin in half and half again to make a small square. Then fold the napkin almost in half again, so that the four free corners almost meet the opposite one.

2 Fold back each corner in turn to come a little lower than the previous one. The shape will now have five graduated points in a line.

3 Fold under the two sides so that the shape is narrower at the base than the top. Tuck one flap into the other at the back.

Left: A plaited straw napkin ring and a posy of wheat transform a plain, pleated napkin into a vibrant harvest decoration.

Simple triangular folds lend themselves to an imaginative presentation, such as the addition of personal gifts and individual candles at each place setting.

1 Fold the napkin with the free end uppermost. Then fold up the right-hand corner so that the point comes half-way up the depth of the rectangle

2 Fold over the napkin along the line created by the previous fold. The bottom and top edges should be parallel.

3 Fold the napkin twice more along each new fold line. Then fold over and tuck in the small flap.

Left: The red paisley patterned handkerchief folded inside the napkin is both practical and pretty. It can be used as a mini hand towel after using a finger bowl.

Pretty napkin rings like this one, a ribbon band partly covered with mimosa and narcissi, could be made to echo the bridal headdresses at a spring wedding.

1 Twist a piece of stiff wire to make a ring. Twist the ends around each other, then bind the ring with narrow ribbon.

2 Cut short lengths of flower sprays such as mimosa and narcissi. Using fine silver wire, bind on the first stems so that the flowers follow the curve of the ring.

3 Bind on more flowers so that each group covers the stem ends of the previous one. Fasten off the wire and carefully arrange the napkin in the ring.

Left: A floral-patterned tablecloth calls for both acknowledgement and restraint in the table decorations. The mini posy of primroses and begonia flowers enhances the stiffened fabric bow.

In a fold representing the rising sun, the white damask napkin is embellished with a posy of golden yellow flowers, contrasting vividly with the traditional blue and white bowls.

1 Fold the napkin in half. Then fold back the top half and fold under the bottom half to make three accordion pleats.

2 Starting at one end of the long rectangle, make even accordion pleats all the way along.

3 Hold the pleats tightly at the base and allow them to fan out loosely at the top. Place the napkin in a shallow bowl or on a plate.

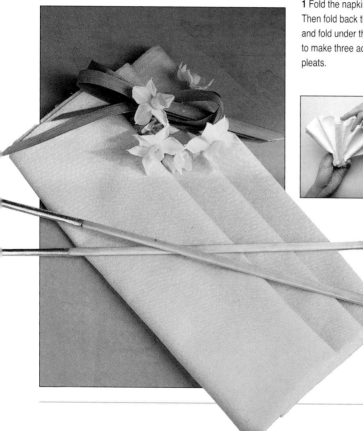

Left: Folded in half and then into three soft folds, the Chinese yellow napkin has a band of knotted iris leaves and sunshine yellow narcissi. Keep the flowers fresh in water until just before the meal is served.

Simplify the service on a picnic or at an informal buffet meal by tucking each place setting of cutlery into a brightly checked napkin folded envelope style.

1 Fold two sides of the napkin to meet in the centre, then fold in the four corners so that the edges meet in the centre.

2 Fold over the two corners to overlap in the centre and form an envelope shape.

3 Turn the napkin over and fold back the two 'open' edges so that they overlap. Tuck one edge inside the other.

Left: A similar presentation can be used on more formal occasions too. A white damask napkin and red carnation set the mood for a stylish dinner party.

Choose your brightest cotton napkins, fold them into stubby candle shapes and partner them with toning beeswax candles to give a festive and co-ordinated look to your Christmas table.

1 Fold the napkin in half diagonally to make a triangle, then fold over the top corners to meet the lower edge.

2 Fold the napkin to bring the upper edge to the centre, then fold back the left-hand side so that its inner edge is vertical.

3 Starting at the left-hand edge, roll the napkin tightly. Tuck the right-hand point under to hold the design in place.

Right: A glittery ribbon bow and a beaded tree ornament add glamour and style to an embroidered napkin folded into graduated pleats.

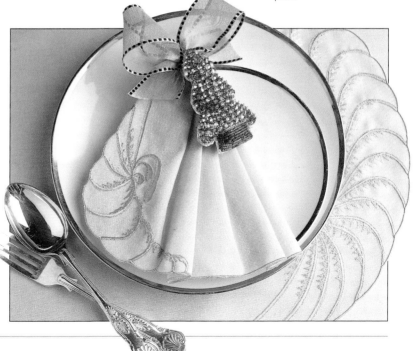

Create an elegant flower container by folding a stiff white napkin into the shape of a rose. The flower stems are held in a small glass bowl in the centre.

1 Fold the four corners to the centre to make a small square, then turn the napkin over and fold the four new corners into the centre.

2 Turn the napkin over again and fold the four new corners to the centre again.

3 Turn the napkin over again, and pull out the folds to make petal shapes. Ease out the folds until they are evenly spaced.

Left: As a variation on the theme, a corn-coloured cotton napkin does decorative duty as a fruit bowl, filled with apricots, lychees and scented geranium leaves.

Make a point of presenting an outdoor meal in country style with sprays of flowers tucked among the multiple folds of a pastel-coloured napkin.

1 Fold the napkin in half and half again, to make a small square. Fold back the top corner.

2 Fold back the next two corners so that the points are at graduating levels.

3 Fold under the two sides so that they are parallel, and press them flat.

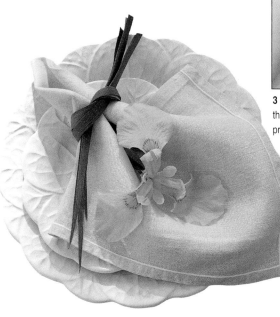

Left: A band of iris leaves knotted around the napkin corner and a bright flower tucked among the folds create a look of planned informality.

Whether you are setting the table for a children's party or at Christmas time, set the scene with these shepherd figures created from rust-coloured napkins and fresh fruits.

1 Fold the napkin in half. Then working from each end in turn, tightly roll it up to the centre.

2 Turn the napkin over and fold it in half with the two rolled sections facing.

3 Lift up one of the rolls and twist it up and over the flat side, like a shawl. Tuck in the end to secure it. Insert a small piece of fruit on a cocktail stick, to represent the head.

Right: You can have all sorts of fun decorating the table with brightly-coloured liquorice sweets. Here they are threaded on to thick black cotton to make irresistible napkin rings.

Get the day off to a good start by setting the breakfast table with textured napkins folded to enclose a boiled or decorated egg.

1 Fold the napkin in half diagonally, to make a triangle, then fold the left- and right-hand corners so that the edges meet in the centre.

2 Turn the napkin over with the loose points at the top. Turn back the lower corner to come about half-way up the diamond shape.

3 Fold the left- and right-hand sides under so that the finished shape slants outwards at the top.

Right: When time is of the essence first thing in the morning, choose bright gingham napkins and flip one corner over the cutlery while another one frames a warm sesame bread roll.

The prettiest and flimsiest of napkins is closely pleated and tied in a knot to represent a bird in flight. The brilliant and exotic border on the plates helps to reinforce the image.

1 Starting at the edge nearest to you, make evenly-spaced accordion pleats along the length of the napkin.

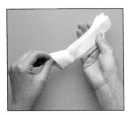

2 Press the pleats firmly in place. Then, holding the napkin at the centre, tie a knot close to one edge.

3 Fan out the pleats to represent a bird's tail. Ease out the lower edges below the knot to neaten the outline.

Below: A cotton napkin in kingfisher blue is
tied in a similar way and presented
swith a brightly coloured
bird decoration and
a spray of
orchids.

Known as the four-feather fold, this napkin design is displayed in a mottled glass goblet and embellished with a cluster of feathers.

1 Fold the napkin in half diagonally to form a triangle, with the folded edge towards you.

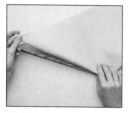

2 Bring the top point over to meet the left-hand corner and fold it so that the lower edge is level with that of the original triangle

3 Bring the next top point over to the left in the same way and fold along the lower edge. Bring the last top point over in a similar way.

4 Fold up the point on the right-hand side. Hold the napkin by that fold and open out the four 'feathers'.

Below: Striking a less formal note, the fold is shown on a printed cotton napkin held in a heavy Mexican glass tumbler. A couple of daisy-like flowerheads echo the second colour in the napkin pattern.

The heavy lace edging on a cream linen napkin is emphasized in this 'breast pocket' fold. The design is well suited to the addition of a pretty hanky or a small gift.

1 Fold the napkin in half and half again to form a small square, with the four free corners facing away from you, then fold it in half diagonally.

2 Turn the napkin over, and fold the top corner down several times to form a thick 'cuff' along the base.

3 Fold down each of the three free points at graduating heights, then fold under the two sides so that the pocket shape is narrower at the base.

Above: In a summery mood, the pocket-shape is
created with a floral-patterned napkin and
embellished with a dainty ribbon-tied posy.

Strike a balance between the formal and casual approach by folding mock-damask paper napkins into a dress-shirt shape. A knotted tartan ribbon tie completes the ensemble.

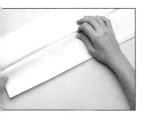

1 Fold the napkin into three, then fold back first the top layer and then the second layer so that the two edges are level with the sides.

2 Fold a short length over at the top. Turn the napkin over and fold back the two top corners at a sharp angle so that they meet in the centre.

3 Fold up the napkin from the base twice, so that the final fold comes level with the 'collar'. Tuck the shirt front under the collar flaps.

Left: It takes two tartan paper napkins placed back to back to create this sartorial about-turn. In this case a gold bow tie provides the finishing touch.

A twist of cotton net and miniature pouches of sugared almonds provide a link with tradition for a place setting at a christening party.

1 To make the bon-bon pouches, cut several circles of net, using a small saucer as a guide.

2 Put three or four layers of net together and place a few almonds in the centre. Draw up the net to enclose them, and tie it with narrow ribbon to make a dolly-bag shape.

3 Cut long strips of net in double thickness and tie them around a rolled napkin. Tie the narrow ribbon around the knot to secure the dolly-bag pouch to the band.

Above: There is no mistaking the 'pink for a girl' theme carried out with this gossamer ribbon bow and its long, sheer trails.

A crisp red napkin with bright green edging is folded into a shape reminiscent of a bishop's hat. A small, bright posy adds a pastoral note.

1 Fold the napkin diagonally to form a triangle. Fold up the two sides so that the edges meet in the centre and form a square.

2 Turn the napkin over, with the free edges facing you. Fold it in half again to form a triangle, then turn it over again.

3 Fold over the two outer corners and tuck one inside the other to secure the shape.

4 Turn the napkin over again and pull down the two side flaps until they are level at the base.

Left: The same only different. In this example, the tricorn headgear has an elegant floral appliqué at its centre and a trail of variegated ivy for contrast.

A white cord ring bound with spiky sprays of rosemary and decorated with star anise - the perfect choice to complement an aromatic main dish.

1 Cut a length of thick white cord and bind the edges together with fine silver wire to make a ring.

2 Bind on short sprays of rosemary half-way round the band, so that the tips of one spray cover the stem ends of the one before.

3 Select as near-perfect star anise pods as possible and stick them at intervals around the ring. Carefully ease the napkin through the band.

Left: A plain rosewood napkin ring is embellished with a decorative bouquet garni of cinnamon, rosemary and bay.

Pleated black moiré ribbon with glittering gold edges is used to emphasize the simulated self-band of this unusual fold.

1 Fold the napkin into three with the free edges uppermost. Roll up the top layer as far as the centre.

2 Turn the napkin over and, starting at one end, roll it up tightly, taking care to keep the outer edges level.

3 Wrap a narrow ribbon band around the centre, to emphasize the simulated band in the napkin fold.

Left: Simplicity is the keynote when the tableware makes a bold design statement. A discreet ribbon bow is all that is needed to enhance the peach-coloured napkin.

Finely pleated and tied at the centre, the napkin is arranged like an extended fan to fill the centre of the underplate.

1 Starting at one end, make evenly-spaced accordion pleats all along the napkin. Press the pleats firmly in place.

2 Fold the pleated napkin in half and tie a ribbon bow around it, just above the fold.

3 Holding the two centre edges together, open out the pleats to form an extended fan shape.

Above: Brightly-coloured wooden beads threaded onto leather thonging are twisted like a bangle around a plain napkin.

A jade-green napkin folded in a two-tier fan shape perfectly complements a plate posy of spring flowers.

1 Fold the napkin in half by folding two opposite edges to the centre.

2 Fold over the lower half to come half-way up the top section and create the two 'tiers'.

3 Starting at one short end, make accordion pleats about 2.5 cm (1 in) wide all along the length. Hold the fan at the base and open out the pleats at the top.

Right: As dainty as any Victorian fan, the shape is created in a lace-trimmed napkin and enhanced with pastel flowers.

Acknowledgements

The author and publishers are grateful to the following for the
loan of the tableware shown throughout the book.

Royal Doulton Ltd
Minton House, London Road
Stoke-on-Trent ST4 7QD
England

Villeroy & Boch tableware
from Saffron Settings
Mercers Row
Saffron Walden
Essex CB10 1HD
England